Stop! Eat!

by Cass Hollander
illustrated by Annette Cable

Scott Foresman

Editorial Offices: Glenview, Illinois • New York, New York
Sales Offices: Reading, Massachusetts • Duluth, Georgia
Glenview, Illinois • Carrollton, Texas • Menlo Park, California

Stop! Eat!

Eat the bugs.

Stop! Eat!

Eat the leaves!

Stop! Eat!

Eat this!

Stop!